M G S

Guiding the black dog home

Helping to understand depression

Contents

1

Introduction

Depression, often referred to as the "black dog," is a pervasive and profound condition that casts a shadow over the lives of millions around the world. Its reach is vast, touching individuals of all ages, backgrounds, and walks of life, weaving a complex tapestry of emotional, psychological, and physical challenges. Yet, despite its prevalence, depression remains widely misunderstood and, all too often, stigmatized.

In "Guiding the Black Dog Home" we aim to illuminate the multifaceted nature of this condition, demystifying the intricacies that underlie its manifestation. Our journey begins with a comprehensive exploration of what depression truly is – beyond the simplified notions and stereotypes that pervade our culture. We delve into the biological, psychological, and social factors that interplay to create the unique experience of everyone who battles this formidable foe.

This book is a culmination of extensive research, personal narratives, and clinical insights designed to provide a holistic understanding of depression. We draw upon the latest scientific advancements to unravel the biological mechanisms that contribute to depressive disorders, exploring the roles of genetics, neurochemistry, and brain structure. Parallel to this, we examine the psychological aspects, including cognitive patterns, emotional regulation, and the impact of trauma and stress.

Recognizing depression as not merely an individual struggle but also a societal issue, we explore the social dimensions that influence mental health. The pressures of modern life, cultural expectations, and socio-economic factors play crucial roles in shaping the prevalence and perception of depression. By acknowledging these broader contexts, we strive to foster a more empathetic and informed approach to supporting those affected.

At its core, this book is a guide – not just for those grappling with depression, but also for their loved ones, caregivers, and anyone seeking to deepen their understanding of this condition. We offer practical strategies and evidence-based therapies that can aid in managing and overcoming depressive episodes. From cognitive-behavioral techniques and mindfulness practices to lifestyle adjustments and pharmacological treatments, our aim is to equip readers with a diverse array of tools and resources.

Moreover, "Guiding the Black Dog Home" is interwoven with poignant personal stories that shed light on the human experience of depression. These narratives, shared with courage and vulnerability, provide a powerful reminder that behind every clinical term and statistic lies a person with a unique story. Through these voices, we hope to break down the barriers of isolation and stigma, fostering a sense of connection and solidarity.

Understanding depression is the first step towards overcoming it. By recognizing the complexity and individuality of this condition, we can pave the way for more effective interventions, compassionate care, and, a brighter future for those affected.

We invite you to embark on this journey with us, to uncover the layers of depression, to challenge misconceptions, and to emerge with a deeper, more nuanced understanding of what it means to truly lead the black dog home.

2

Understanding Depression

Depression is a pervasive mental health issue that impacts individuals across the globe, manifesting in various forms and intensities. It is characterized by a persistent low mood, loss of interest in daily activities, and a wide array of physical and emotional symptoms that can significantly impair one's ability to function. The condition transcends mere sadness, often becoming a debilitating state that affects eating, sleeping, and the overall quality of life. Understanding depression involves recognizing its complexity, acknowledging the spectrum of depressive disorders, and appreciating the individual experiences of those affected.

Depression can present as major depressive disorder, persistent depressive disorder, seasonal affective disorder, and perinatal depression, among others. Each type has unique features, but common symptoms include feelings of emptiness, hopelessness, and a pervasive sense of fatigue. The causes of depression are equally multifaceted, involving genetic, biological, environmental, and psychological factors. Treatment options vary and can include medication, psychotherapy, lifestyle changes, and support groups, tailored to the individual's needs.

Awareness and education about depression are crucial in fostering understanding and empathy. It is important to dispel myths and misconceptions that contribute to the stigma surrounding mental health. Support from family, friends, and mental health professionals plays a vital role in the recovery process. Moreover, self-care practices and seeking help when needed are essential steps in managing depression.

As society progresses in its understanding of mental health, it is imperative to continue research, improve access to care, and advocate for those living with depression. By doing so, we can create a more inclusive environment where individuals feel empowered to seek help and support for their mental well-being.

3

The Personal Battle

Depression is a deeply personal experience, a shadow that lurks in the corners of one's mind, altering perceptions and emotions in ways that are often difficult to articulate. While the clinical aspects of depression provide a framework for understanding, the true essence of this condition is found in the stories of those who live through it. In this chapter, we share personal anecdotes from individuals who have bravely faced the black dog, each story a testament to the unique and multifaceted nature of depression.

Sarah's Story: The Invisible Weight

For Sarah, depression came like a slow-moving fog, gradually obscuring her vibrant personality and zest for life. A successful graphic designer in her early thirties, Sarah was known for her creativity and enthusiasm. But one day, she woke up feeling inexplicably drained. What started as occasional bouts of sadness soon morphed into a constant, oppressive weight.

"I remember staring at my computer screen, unable to muster the energy to move the mouse," she recalls. "It felt like there was an invisible force holding me down, making even the simplest tasks seem insurmountable."

Despite her internal struggle, Sarah kept her pain hidden from her colleagues and friends. She feared being judged or misunderstood. "People always saw me as the cheerful one, the problem solver. Admitting that I was struggling felt like admitting defeat."

Sarah's turning point came when she confided in her close friend, Emily, who gently urged her to seek professional help. "It was the hardest conversation I've ever had, but it was also the most important. Therapy helped me understand that depression is not a weakness. It's an illness, and it's okay to ask for help."

James' Journey: The Mask of Perfection

James, a high-achieving law student, wore the mask of perfection with ease. To the outside world, he was the epitome of success – top of his class, captain of the debate team, and a future star in the legal field. But beneath the surface, James was battling a relentless wave of self-doubt and despair.

"I felt like an imposter, constantly terrified that I would be exposed as a fraud," James admits. "No matter how much I accomplished, it was never enough to silence the critical voice in my head."

James' depression manifested as severe anxiety and perfectionism, pushing him to work tirelessly, often at the expense of his health and relationships. "I was afraid to slow down, fearing that if I stopped, everything would fall apart."

The breaking point came during his second year of law school when James experienced a panic attack during a moot court competition. "I felt like I was drowning, gasping for air while the world watched in slow motion."

It was this harrowing experience that led James to seek help. Through a combination of therapy and medication, he learned to manage his anxiety and set realistic expectations for himself. "It's a continuous journey, but I've learned that vulnerability is not a sign of weakness. It's a strength."

Lila's Battle: The Silent Scream

For Lila, depression was a silent scream, a cry for help that seemed to echo unheard through the halls of her mind. As a teenager, Lila struggled with feelings of worthlessness and isolation, exacerbated by the pressures of social media and academic performance.

"Every time I scrolled through my feed, it felt like a parade of everyone else's perfect lives," Lila shares. "I couldn't help but compare myself and feel like I was falling short in every way."

Lila's depression led to self-harm, a desperate attempt to externalize the pain she felt inside. "It was the only way I knew how to cope. The physical pain was a distraction from the emotional agony."

A concerned teacher noticed the signs and reached out, guiding Lila to seek help from the school counsellor. "That small act of kindness changed everything. It made me realize that I wasn't alone and that there were people who cared."

Through counselling and support groups, Lila began to rebuild her self-esteem and find healthier ways to cope with her emotions. "It's a daily battle, but I've learned to be kinder to myself and to reach out when I need support."

Ahmed's Struggle: The Cultural Stigma

Ahmed's experience with depression was compounded by cultural stigma and expectations. Growing up in a close-knit immigrant family, Ahmed felt immense pressure to succeed and uphold his family's honour. However, the weight of these expectations took a toll on his mental health.

"In my culture, mental health issues are often seen as a sign of weakness or failure," Ahmed explains. "Admitting that I was struggling felt like I was letting everyone down."

Ahmed's depression manifested as chronic fatigue and a sense of numbness. He withdrew from social activities and found it increasingly difficult to engage with his studies. "It felt like I was walking through a thick fog, unable to see the path ahead."

A compassionate professor noticed Ahmed's decline and offered a listening ear. "He didn't judge or lecture me. He just listened, and that made all the difference."

With the professor's encouragement, Ahmed sought help from a therapist who understood the cultural nuances of his experience. "Therapy helped me navigate the complex interplay between my cultural identity and my mental health. It was liberating to realize that I could seek help without betraying my heritage."

Maria's Triumph: Rediscovering Joy

Maria's battle with depression began after the birth of her second child. What should have been a joyous time was overshadowed by a deep and pervasive sadness. "I loved my children, but I felt disconnected and overwhelmed. The guilt was crushing."

Postpartum depression robbed Maria of the simple joys of motherhood. She felt isolated and ashamed, fearing that she would be judged as a bad mother. "I kept telling myself that I should be happy, but the darkness was all-consuming."

With the support of her husband and a compassionate healthcare provider, Maria sought treatment for postpartum depression. "It was a difficult journey, but therapy and support groups helped me realize that I wasn't alone and that my feelings didn't define my worth as a mother."

Through her recovery, Maria rediscovered the joy of

motherhood and learned to prioritize her own well-being. "It's an ongoing process, but I've learned that taking care of myself is not selfish. It's essential for me and my family."

Conclusion

The stories of Sarah, James, Lila, Ahmed, and Maria are just a few of the countless personal battles fought against depression every day. Each story is unique, highlighting the diverse ways in which depression can manifest and the varied paths to recovery.

By sharing these personal anecdotes, we hope to shed light on the human experience of depression and foster a deeper understanding of this complex condition. Depression is not a one-size-fits-all illness; it is a deeply personal journey, shaped by individual experiences, cultural backgrounds, and life circumstances.

Through empathy, support, and a commitment to destigmatizing mental health, we can create a world where those battling the black dog can find the strength to persevere and the hope to heal.

4

The Role of Support

Depression, with its pervasive and often debilitating effects, is not a battle that should be fought alone. The role of a dedicated support system is crucial in the journey toward recovery and well-being. Friends, family, and healthcare professionals form a network of care that can provide the understanding, compassion, and resources needed to navigate the complexities of depression. In this chapter, we explore the significance of each component of this support system and how they collectively contribute to the healing process.

Friends: The First Line of Defence

Friends often serve as the first line of defence against depression. They are the ones who notice the subtle changes in behaviour, the quiet withdrawal, and the unspoken cries for help. A supportive friend can make a profound difference in the life of someone struggling with depression.

Recognizing the Signs

One of the key role's friends play is recognizing the signs of depression. This includes noticing when a friend seems unusually sad, anxious, or fatigued; when they withdraw from social activities; or when they express feelings of hopelessness. Friends who are observant and compassionate can provide the first indication that something is amiss.

Offering Support

Support from friends can take many forms, from simply being there to listen without judgment to encouraging their friend to seek professional help. Sometimes, offering practical help—like accompanying them to appointments or helping with daily tasks—can alleviate some of the burden they are carrying.

Being Patient and Understanding

It's important for friends to be patient and understanding. Depression can be a long and arduous journey, and those affected may not always respond to offers of help immediately. Friends need to remain steadfast, providing consistent support and reminding their friend that they are not alone.

Family: The Pillars of Strength

Family members are often deeply affected when a loved one is battling depression. Their role is pivotal in providing a stable and nurturing environment that fosters recovery.

Creating a Supportive Home Environment

A supportive home environment is essential for someone dealing with depression. Family members can contribute by creating a safe space where the individual feels loved and accepted. This includes being attentive to their needs, offering encouragement, and avoiding criticism or blame.

Educating Themselves

Family members should educate themselves about depression to better understand what their loved one is going through. Knowledge about the condition, its symptoms, and its treatment can help them provide more effective support and reduce feelings of frustration or helplessness.

Encouraging Professional Help

While family support is crucial, it is not a substitute for professional help. Family members should encourage their loved one to seek therapy or medication if needed and support them in following through with their treatment plan.

Taking Care of Themselves

Caring for someone with depression can be emotionally taxing.

Family members need to take care of their own mental health and seek support when necessary. This might include joining support groups, seeking counselling, or simply taking time for self-care.

Healthcare Professionals: The Expert Guides

Healthcare professionals play an indispensable role in diagnosing, treating, and managing depression. Their expertise provides the foundation for a comprehensive treatment plan tailored to the individual's needs.

Therapists and Counsellors

Therapists and counsellors are trained to help individuals understand and manage their depression. Through various forms of therapy, such as cognitive-behavioural therapy (CBT), psychotherapy, or counselling, they provide tools and strategies to cope with depressive symptoms and address underlying issues.

Psychiatrists

Psychiatrists, as medical doctors specializing in mental health, can prescribe medications that can help alleviate the symptoms of depression. They work closely with patients to find the right medication and dosage, monitoring for side effects and making adjustments as needed.

Primary Care Physicians

Primary care physicians often serve as the first point of contact in the healthcare system. They can screen for depression, provide initial support, and refer patients to mental health specialists. Their role is crucial in the early detection and intervention of depression.

Support Groups and Peer Support

Support groups and peer support play a complementary role in the treatment of depression. These groups provide a space for individuals to share their experiences, offer mutual support, and learn from others who have faced similar challenges. The sense of community and understanding found in support groups can be immensely therapeutic.

The Synergy of Support

The constructive collaboration between friends, family, and healthcare professionals creates a comprehensive support system that addresses the multifaceted nature of depression. Each component plays a unique and essential role, contributing to the overall well-being of the individual.

Building a Network

Building a dedicated support network involves open

communication and collaboration among all parties involved. Friends and family should stay informed about the individual's treatment plan and progress, while healthcare professionals should encourage the involvement of loved ones in the recovery process.

Empowering the Individual

The goal of a support system is to empower the individual to take an active role in their own recovery. This includes encouraging them to participate in therapy, adhere to their treatment plan, and engage in self-care practices. Empowerment fosters a sense of control and agency, which is crucial for overcoming depression.

Celebrating Progress

Recovery from depression is often a gradual process marked by small victories and setbacks. It's important for the support system to celebrate progress, no matter how small, and provide encouragement during challenging times. Recognizing and validating the individual's efforts can boost their motivation and resilience.

Conclusion

The battle against depression is a formidable one, but it is not a fight that must be waged alone. A dedicated support system comprising friends, family, and healthcare professionals provides the foundation for recovery and healing. By recognizing the signs, offering unwavering support, and encouraging professional help, loved ones can make a profound difference in the lives of those struggling with depression.

The journey to overcoming depression is a collective effort, one that requires compassion, understanding, and collaboration. Together, we can create a world where the shadows of depression are met with the light of hope, resilience, and enduring support.

5

Treatment and Therapy

Depression, with its diverse manifestations and profound impact on daily life, requires a comprehensive and personalized approach to treatment. No single treatment fits all, and the journey toward finding what works best for each person can be as unique as the individuals themselves. In this chapter, we delve into various treatment options, including medication, therapy, and alternative treatments, providing a road map for those seeking to manage and overcome depression.

Understanding Treatment Approaches

The treatment of depression typically involves a combination of approaches, each targeting different aspects of the condition. These approaches can be broadly categorized into pharmacological treatments, psychotherapy, and alternative therapies. The choice of treatment depends on the severity of the depression, individual preferences, and specific needs.

Antidepressant Medications

Antidepressant medications are often a cornerstone of depression treatment, particularly for moderate to severe cases. They work by altering brain chemistry to improve mood and alleviate depressive symptoms. There are several types of antidepressants, each with distinct mechanisms of action:

1. **Selective Serotonin Re-uptake Inhibitors (SSRIs)**: SSRIs, such as fluoxetine (Prozac) and sertraline (Zoloft), are commonly prescribed due to their effectiveness and mild side effect profile. They increase serotonin levels in the brain, which helps improve mood and emotional stability.

2. **Serotonin-Norepinephrine Re-uptake Inhibitors (SNRIs)**: SNRIs, such as venlafaxine (Effexor) and duloxetine (Cymbalta), target both serotonin and norepinephrine, two neurotransmitters involved in mood regulation. They are often used when SSRIs are not effective.

3. **Tricyclic Antidepressants (TCAs)**: TCAs, such as amitriptyline and nortriptyline, are older medications that can be effective but often have more side effects. They are typically used when newer antidepressants are ineffective.

4. **Monoamine Oxidase Inhibitors (MAOIs)**: MAOIs, such as phenelzine (Nardil) and tranylcypromine (Parnate), are another older class of antidepressants. They are usually reserved for cases that do not respond to other treatments due to their potential for serious dietary and drug interactions.

5. **Atypical Antidepressants**: This category includes medications like bupropion (Wellbutrin) and mirtazapine (Remeron), which work through different mechanisms and can be useful for individuals who do not respond to or cannot tolerate other antidepressants.

Finding the Right Medication

Finding the right antidepressant can be a process of trial and error. It often involves adjusting dosages and trying different medications to achieve the desired effect with minimal side effects. Close collaboration with a healthcare provider is essential during this process.

Augmentation Strategies

In some cases, additional medications, such as mood stabilizers or antipsychotics, may be added to enhance the effectiveness of antidepressants. These augmentation strategies can be particularly helpful for individuals with treatment-resistant depression.

Psychotherapy

Psychotherapy, or talk therapy, is a fundamental component of depression treatment. It involves working with a trained therapist to address the emotional and psychological aspects of depression. There are several types of psychotherapy, each with its own approach and techniques:

Cognitive-Behavioural Therapy (CBT)

CBT is one of the most widely used therapies for depression. It focuses on identifying and changing negative thought patterns and behaviours that contribute to depressive symptoms. Through CBT, individuals learn to challenge distorted thinking, develop healthier coping mechanisms, and build resilience.

Interpersonal Therapy (IPT)

IPT addresses the interpersonal and social factors that can contribute to depression. It focuses on improving communication skills, resolving conflicts, and building supportive relationships. IPT is particularly effective for individuals whose depression is linked to relationship issues or life transitions.

Psychodynamic Therapy

Psychodynamic therapy explores the underlying psychological roots of depression, often stemming from past experiences and unresolved conflicts. It aims to increase self-awareness and understanding of how these factors influence current behaviour and emotions.

Mindfulness-Based Cognitive Therapy (MBCT)

MBCT combines principles of cognitive therapy with mindfulness practices. It teaches individuals to become more aware of their thoughts and feelings in the present moment, reducing the risk of relapse by breaking the cycle of negative thinking.

Dialectical Behaviour Therapy (DBT)

Originally developed for borderline personality disorder, DBT has been adapted for depression treatment. It combines cognitive-behavioural techniques with mindfulness and acceptance strategies, helping individuals regulate emotions and tolerate distress.

Finding the Right Therapist

Choosing the right therapist and therapy type is crucial for effective treatment. It may take time to find a therapist with whom the individual feels comfortable and whose approach aligns with their needs and preferences.

Alternative and Complementary Treatments

In addition to medication and psychotherapy, several alternative and complementary treatments can support the management of depression. These approaches can be used alongside traditional treatments to enhance overall well-being.

Exercise

Regular physical activity has been shown to have a positive

impact on mood and can be an effective way to alleviate mild to moderate depressive symptoms. Exercise promotes the release of endorphins and other neurotransmitters that enhance mood and reduce stress.

Nutrition

A healthy diet can play a significant role in mental health. Nutrient-rich foods that support brain function, such as those high in omega-3 fatty acids, vitamins, and minerals, can help improve mood and energy levels.

Sleep Hygiene

Good sleep hygiene practices are essential for managing depression. Establishing a regular sleep routine, creating a comfortable sleep environment, and avoiding stimulants before bedtime can improve sleep quality and overall mental health.

Mindfulness and Meditation

Mindfulness and meditation practices can help individuals manage stress, reduce anxiety, and improve emotional regulation. These practices promote a state of calm and focus, which can be beneficial for those struggling with depression.

Acupuncture

Some individuals find relief from depressive symptoms through acupuncture, an ancient Chinese practice that involves inserting thin needles into specific points on the body. While research on its effectiveness is ongoing, acupuncture is believed to help balance the body's energy flow and promote well-being.

Herbal Supplements

Certain herbal supplements, such as St. John's wort and SAMe, have been studied for their potential antidepressant effects. However, it is essential to consult with a healthcare provider before using these supplements, as they can interact with other medications and have side effects.

The Journey to Recovery

The journey to recovery from depression is often non-linear, with difficulties along the way. Finding the right combination of treatments can take time and requires patience, persistence, and a willingness to explore different options. Here are some key considerations for individuals on this journey:

Personalized Treatment Plans

Every individual's experience with depression is unique, and treatment plans should be tailored to their specific needs and circumstances. A comprehensive assessment by a healthcare professional can help determine the most appropriate treatment approach.

Open Communication

Open and honest communication with healthcare providers is essential for effective treatment. Individuals should feel comfortable discussing their symptoms, treatment preferences, and any concerns or side effects they experience.

Support Networks

A dedicated support network of friends, family, and healthcare professionals can provide the encouragement and assistance needed to navigate the challenges of depression. Support groups and peer networks can also offer valuable insights and a sense of community.

Self-Care and Resilience

Self-care practices, such as maintaining a healthy lifestyle, engaging in enjoyable activities, and practicing stress management techniques, are vital components of depression treatment. Building resilience through positive coping strategies can enhance overall well-being.

Hope and Patience

Recovery from depression takes time, and setbacks are a natural part of the process. Maintaining hope and patience, and celebrating small victories along the way, can help individuals stay motivated and committed to their treatment journey.

Conclusion

Treatment and therapy for depression encompass a wide range of approaches, from medication and psychotherapy to alternative and complementary treatments. The journey to finding what works best is highly individual and may require a combination of methods to achieve optimal results. By exploring different options, maintaining open communication with healthcare providers, and leveraging the support of loved ones, individuals can navigate the complexities of depression and move toward a brighter, healthier future.

6

The Power of Resilience

Resilience is the remarkable capacity to withstand adversity, bounce back from difficult experiences, and emerge stronger. For those battling depression, resilience is not just a trait; it is a lifeline. The journey through depression is often fraught with challenges, setbacks, and moments of profound struggle. Yet, amidst this darkness, the strength and resilience shown by individuals in their quest for recovery are nothing short of extraordinary. This chapter celebrates that resilience and explores how it manifests, is nurtured, and leads to recovery.

Understanding Resilience

Resilience is the ability to adapt and thrive despite adversity. It involves a combination of inner strengths and external resources that help individuals navigate the complexities of life. Resilience is not about avoiding difficulties but rather about facing them with courage and perseverance. For those with depression, resilience can mean the difference between feeling overwhelmed by their condition and finding the strength to seek help and pursue recovery.

The Nature of Resilience in Depression

Depression can feel like an insurmountable mountain, casting a shadow over every aspect of life. Resilience in the context of depression involves several key components:

1. **Adaptability**: The ability to adjust one's thoughts, emotions, and behaviours in response to changing circumstances.
2. **Optimism**: Maintaining a hopeful outlook and believing in the possibility of improvement, even when faced with setbacks.
3. **Self-Efficacy**: A belief in one's ability to influence outcomes and make positive changes in life.
4. **Social Support**: Leveraging relationships with friends, family, and support networks to provide strength and encouragement.
5. **Problem-Solving Skills**: The capacity to identify challenges and develop effective strategies to address them.

Stories of Resilience

The power of resilience is best illustrated through the stories of those who have confronted their depression and worked towards recovery. These narratives highlight the diverse ways in which resilience can manifest and the profound impact it can have on individuals' lives.

Anna's Story: Finding Light in Darkness

Anna, a schoolteacher in her forties, had always been known for her cheerful demeanour and dedication to her students. However, after a series of personal losses, she found herself sinking into a deep depression. The once vibrant classrooms now seemed grey and lifeless, mirroring her internal state.

"I felt like I was drowning," Anna recalls. "Every day was a struggle just to get out of bed."

Despite the overwhelming despair, Anna decided to seek help. She started seeing a therapist who introduced her to cognitive-behavioural therapy (CBT). Through CBT, Anna learned to identify and challenge the negative thoughts that fuelled her depression. She also began practicing mindfulness, which helped her stay present and find moments of peace.

"Therapy was a turning point for me," Anna says. "It didn't happen overnight, but slowly, I started to feel like myself again. The support from my therapist and my determination to get better kept me going."

Anna's resilience was further bolstered by her passion for teaching. She found solace and purpose in her work, which became a source of motivation and joy. Today, Anna continues to teach, using her experience with depression to empathize with and support her students who may be struggling.

Michael's Journey: Rebuilding a Life

Michael, a former athlete, experienced depression after a career-ending injury. The loss of his identity as an athlete left him feeling directionless and despondent. The physical pain of his injury was compounded by the emotional pain of losing his dream.

"For a long time, I felt like I had nothing to live for," Michael admits. "I was angry, bitter, and deeply depressed."

With the encouragement of a close friend, Michael sought help from a mental health professional. He was introduced to a combination of medication and psychotherapy, which helped stabilize his mood and address the underlying issues contributing to his depression.

Michael also found new ways to channel his energy and passion. He began volunteering at a community centre, coaching young athletes. This new role allowed him to reconnect with his love for sports and make a positive impact on others.

"Coaching gave me a new sense of purpose," Michael reflects. "It helped me see that while my career as an athlete was over, I could still contribute in meaningful ways."

Michael's resilience was evident in his ability to adapt to his new circumstances and find fulfilment in a different capacity. His journey underscores the importance of finding new avenues for passion and purpose in the face of loss.

Sophia's Battle: The Strength of Vulnerability

Sophia, a young artist, faced depression during her college years. The pressures of academic life, combined with personal insecurities, led to feelings of worthlessness and isolation. Sophia struggled to share her feelings with others, fearing judgment and misunderstanding.

"I felt like a burden," Sophia recalls. "I didn't want to bring anyone down with my problems."

Sophia's breakthrough came when she decided to confide in a trusted professor. This act of vulnerability opened the door to a network of support. Her professor connected her with counselling services, and Sophia began attending regular therapy sessions.

Through therapy, Sophia learned to embrace her vulnerability as a strength rather than a weakness. She began to express her emotions through her art, which became a powerful outlet for her pain and a means of connecting with others.

"Art was my lifeline," Sophia explains. "It allowed me to process my emotions and share my journey with others. The support I received from my professor, therapist, and friends was invaluable."

Sophia's resilience was rooted in her willingness to be vulnerable and seek help. Her story highlights the transformative power of creative expression and the importance of reaching out for support.

Nurturing Resilience

Resilience is not a fixed trait but a dynamic quality that can be cultivated and strengthened. Here are some strategies to nurture resilience in the face of depression:

1. Building Strong Relationships

Social connections are a cornerstone of resilience. Cultivating supportive relationships with friends, family, and community members provides a network of care and encouragement. Engaging in meaningful social activities and seeking support when needed can fortify one's resilience.

2. Developing Coping Skills

Effective coping skills are essential for managing stress and adversity. Techniques such as mindfulness, meditation, deep breathing exercises, and journaling can help individuals regulate their emotions and maintain a sense of calm during challenging times.

3. Setting Realistic Goals

Setting achievable goals provides a sense of purpose and direction. Breaking larger goals into smaller, manageable steps can create a sense of accomplishment and momentum, reinforcing resilience.

4. Practicing Self-Compassion

Self-compassion involves treating oneself with kindness and understanding during times of difficulty. It means acknowledging one's struggles without self-judgment and recognizing that setbacks are a natural part of the recovery process.

5. Embracing Flexibility

Flexibility is the ability to adapt to changing circumstances and remain open to new possibilities. Embracing flexibility allows individuals to navigate life's uncertainties with greater ease and resilience.

6. Fostering a Positive Outlook

Maintaining a positive outlook does not mean ignoring difficulties but rather focusing on strengths and possibilities. Practices such as gratitude journaling and positive affirmations can help shift one's perspective and build optimism.

The Impact of Resilience

The impact of resilience extends beyond individual recovery. Resilient individuals often inspire and support others facing similar challenges, creating a ripple effect of strength and hope. By sharing their stories and strategies, they contribute to a culture of empathy and understanding, reducing the stigma surrounding mental health.

Conclusion

The power of resilience is a testament to the human spirit's ability to overcome adversity and emerge stronger. For those confronting depression, resilience is a vital force that fuels the journey toward recovery. By nurturing resilience through strong relationships, effective coping skills, self-compassion, and a positive outlook, individuals can navigate the complexities of depression and reclaim their lives.

The stories of Anna, Michael, Sophia, and countless others remind us that resilience is not about being invincible but about rising after every fall. Their journeys inspire us to recognize the strength within ourselves and to support one another in the collective fight against depression. Together, we celebrate the resilience that illuminates the path from darkness to light.

7

Lifestyle Changes

Depression is a multifaceted condition that affects both the mind and body. While medication and therapy are critical components of treatment, lifestyle changes can significantly impact mental health and enhance the overall well-being of individuals struggling with depression. In this chapter, we explore the influence of exercise, diet, and sleep patterns on mental health and how incorporating positive lifestyle changes can support the journey toward recovery.

The Connection Between Lifestyle and Mental Health

The relationship between lifestyle and mental health is complex and interconnected. Physical health and mental health are deeply intertwined, and changes in one can significantly affect the other. Making positive lifestyle changes can help alleviate symptoms of depression, improve mood, and enhance resilience. Let's delve into the specific areas where lifestyle changes can make a difference.

Exercise: The Natural Antidepressant

Exercise is often referred to as nature's antidepressant, and for a good reason. Physical activity has numerous benefits for mental health, including:

1. **Releasing Endorphins**: Exercise stimulates the production of endorphins, the body's natural mood elevators. These chemicals help reduce pain and increase feelings of pleasure and well-being.

2. **Reducing Stress**: Physical activity helps lower cortisol levels, the hormone associated with stress. Lowering stress can improve overall mood and reduce anxiety.

3. **Improving Sleep**: Regular exercise can regulate sleep patterns, leading to better quality sleep. Improved sleep has a direct positive impact on mental health.

4. **Boosting Self-Esteem**: Engaging in regular physical activity can enhance self-esteem and body image, contributing to a more positive outlook on life.

5. **Providing a Sense of Accomplishment**: Setting and achieving fitness goals, no matter how small, can provide a sense of accomplishment and boost confidence.

Incorporating Exercise into Daily Life

The key to reaping the mental health benefits of exercise is consistency. Here are some tips for incorporating physical activity into daily life:

- **Start Small**: Begin with short, manageable activities such as a 10-minute walk and gradually increase the duration and intensity.
- **Choose Enjoyable Activities**: Engage in activities that you enjoy, whether it's dancing, swimming, cycling, or yoga. This increases the likelihood of maintaining a regular exercise routine.
- **Create a Routine**: Schedule exercise at a specific time each day to build a habit. Consistency is crucial for long-term benefits.
- **Find a Workout Buddy**: Exercising with a friend can provide motivation, accountability, and social interaction.
- **Mix It Up**: Variety keeps exercise interesting. Alternate between several types of activities to prevent boredom.

Diet: Nourishing the Mind and Body

Nutrition plays a crucial role in mental health. A balanced diet provides the essential nutrients needed for brain function, energy, and mood regulation. Certain dietary choices can either exacerbate or alleviate symptoms of depression.

The Role of Nutrients in Mental Health

- **Omega-3 Fatty Acids**: Found in fatty fish, flaxseeds, and walnuts, omega-3 fatty acids are essential for brain health. They have been shown to reduce inflammation and support

neurotransmitter function, potentially alleviating depressive symptoms.
- **Vitamins and Minerals**: B vitamins (such as B6, B12, and folate), vitamin D, magnesium, and zinc are crucial for brain function and mood regulation. Deficiencies in these nutrients can contribute to depressive symptoms.
- **Antioxidants**: Foods rich in antioxidants, such as fruits and vegetables, help combat oxidative stress, which can affect mental health.

Creating a Mood-Boosting Diet

To optimize mental health through diet, consider the following strategies:

- **Eat a Balanced Diet**: Include a variety of fruits, vegetables, whole grains, lean proteins, and healthy fats in your diet. This ensures you receive a wide range of nutrients necessary for overall health.
- **Limit Processed Foods**: Reduce the intake of processed foods, sugary snacks, and refined carbohydrates, which can lead to mood swings and energy crashes.
- **Stay Hydrated**: Dehydration can affect mood and cognitive function. Aim to drink plenty of water throughout the day.
- **Monitor Caffeine and Alcohol Intake**: While moderate caffeine consumption can boost alertness, excessive intake can lead to anxiety and sleep disturbances. Similarly, alcohol can disrupt sleep and exacerbate depressive symptoms.
- **Consider Supplements**: If it's challenging to get certain nutrients from your diet alone, consider supplements after

consulting with a healthcare provider.

Sleep: The Foundation of Mental Health

Adequate sleep is essential for maintaining mental health. Sleep disturbances are common in individuals with depression, and improving sleep quality can significantly enhance mood and overall well-being.

The Impact of Sleep on Mental Health

- **Mood Regulation**: Sleep helps regulate mood by allowing the brain to process emotions and experiences. Poor sleep can lead to irritability, anxiety, and increased sensitivity to stress.
- **Cognitive Function**: Sleep is crucial for cognitive processes such as memory, learning, and problem-solving. Lack of sleep can impair these functions and contribute to feelings of confusion and frustration.
- **Physical Health**: Adequate sleep supports physical health by boosting the immune system, reducing inflammation, and promoting cardiovascular health. Physical well-being, in turn, supports mental health.

Improving Sleep Hygiene

Good sleep hygiene involves creating an environment and routine conducive to restful sleep. Here are some tips to improve sleep quality:

- **Establish a Routine**: Go to bed and wake up at the same time every day, even on weekends, to regulate your body's internal clock.
- **Create a Relaxing Bedtime Routine**: Engage in calming activities before bed, such as reading, taking a warm bath, or practicing relaxation techniques.
- **Limit Screen Time**: Reduce exposure to screens (phones, tablets, computers) at least an hour before bed. The blue light emitted by screens can interfere with the production of melatonin, the sleep hormone.
- **Create a Sleep-Friendly Environment**: Ensure your bedroom is cool, dark, and quiet. Use comfortable bedding and eliminate noise and light disruptions.
- **Avoid Stimulants**: Limit caffeine and nicotine intake, especially in the evening. These stimulants can interfere with falling and staying asleep.
- **Be Mindful of Food and Drink**: Avoid large meals, spicy foods, and heavy drinking close to bedtime. These can cause discomfort and disrupt sleep.

Combining Lifestyle Changes for Maximum Impact

While each lifestyle change can independently benefit mental health, their combined effects can be even more powerful. Integrating exercise, a balanced diet, and good sleep hygiene into your daily routine can create a synergistic effect, enhancing overall well-being and supporting recovery from depression.

Creating a Holistic Routine

1. **Morning Routine**:
- **Exercise**: Start the day with a brisk walk, yoga, or any preferred physical activity to boost endorphins and energy levels.
- **Healthy Breakfast**: Eat a nutritious breakfast that includes whole grains, protein, and healthy fats to fuel your brain and body.

2. **Daytime Routine**:
- **Balanced Meals**: Consume balanced meals throughout the day, incorporating a variety of nutrients.
- **Hydration**: Drink water regularly to stay hydrated.
- **Mindfulness Breaks**: Take short breaks to practice mindfulness or deep breathing, reducing stress and enhancing focus.

3. **Evening Routine**:
- **Relaxing Activities**: Engage in relaxing activities such as reading, listening to music, or taking a warm bath.
- **Light Dinner**: Have a light dinner, avoiding heavy or spicy foods.
- **Limit Screen Time**: Reduce exposure to screens an hour before bed to promote melatonin production.

4. **Bedtime Routine**:
- **Consistent Sleep Schedule**: Go to bed at the same time each night to regulate your sleep cycle.
- **Sleep Environment**: Ensure your bedroom is conducive to sleep by keeping it cool, dark, and quiet.

Overcoming Challenges

Making lifestyle changes can be challenging, especially when dealing with depression. Here are some strategies to overcome common obstacles:

- **Set Realistic Goals**: Start with small, achievable goals and gradually build on them. This approach prevents overwhelm and encourages steady progress.
- **Seek Support**: Enlist the help of friends, family, or a support group to provide encouragement and accountability.
- **Be Patient**: Understand that change takes time. Celebrate small victories and be compassionate with yourself during setbacks.
- **Stay Flexible**: Adapt your routine as needed. If a particular strategy isn't working, try a different approach.

Conclusion

Lifestyle changes, including exercise, diet, and sleep patterns, play a crucial role in managing depression and enhancing mental health. By incorporating these changes into daily life, individuals can create a foundation of physical and emotional well-being that supports recovery and resilience.

The journey to improved mental health through lifestyle changes is deeply personal and unique to everyone. It requires patience, persistence, and a willingness to explore different strategies. However, the benefits are profound, leading to a healthier, more balanced life and a brighter outlook on the future.

Embracing these lifestyle changes empowers individuals to take an active role in their mental health journey, complementing traditional treatments and fostering a comprehensive approach to recovery. Through consistent effort and support, the path to mental well-being becomes clearer and more attainable.

8

The Stigma of Depression

Depression, despite being one of the most common mental health conditions, is often surrounded by a significant amount of stigma. This stigma can manifest in numerous ways, from misunderstanding and discrimination to social exclusion. Addressing the societal stigma associated with depression is crucial for fostering a culture of empathy, understanding, and support. In this chapter, we will explore the origins and impacts of stigma, share personal stories that highlight these challenges, and advocate for greater awareness and acceptance.

Understanding Stigma

Stigma refers to the negative attitudes, beliefs, and behaviours directed towards individuals who have a particular characteristic or condition. In the context of depression, stigma often arises from misconceptions and a lack of awareness about mental health. This stigma can be categorized into three main types:

1. **Public Stigma**: The negative or discriminatory attitudes that society holds towards people with depression.
2. **Self-Stigma**: The internalization of these negative attitudes by individuals with depression, leading to feelings of shame and low self-worth.
3. **Institutional Stigma**: Policies and practices within institutions (such as workplaces, schools, and healthcare systems) that systematically discriminate against people with depression.

The Origins of Stigma

Stigma surrounding depression has deep-rooted origins, often stemming from historical, cultural, and social factors:

1. **Historical Misunderstandings**: Historically, mental illness was poorly understood and often attributed to moral failings or supernatural forces. These misconceptions have lingered, contributing to ongoing stigma.
2. **Cultural Attitudes**: Different cultures have varying attitudes towards mental health. In some cultures, discussing mental health issues is taboo, and seeking help is seen as a sign of weakness.
3. **Media Representations**: Media portrayals of mental illness can perpetuate stereotypes and misinformation. Negative or sensationalized depictions of depression can reinforce stigma and fear.
4. **Lack of Education**: A general lack of education and awareness about mental health contributes to

misunderstanding and stigma. People may not realize that depression is a medical condition that requires treatment and support.

The Impact of Stigma

The stigma associated with depression can have profound and far-reaching effects on individuals and society:

1. **Barriers to Seeking Help**: Fear of being judged or discriminated against can prevent individuals from seeking the help they need. This can lead to untreated depression and worsening symptoms.
2. **Social Isolation**: Stigma can lead to social exclusion, where individuals with depression feel isolated from their communities, friends, and family.
3. **Workplace Discrimination**: People with depression may face discrimination in the workplace, affecting their job prospects, career advancement, and overall job satisfaction.
4. **Internalized Shame**: Self-stigma can lead to feelings of guilt, shame, and worthlessness. This internalized stigma can exacerbate depressive symptoms and hinder recovery.
5. **Healthcare Disparities**: Institutional stigma can result in unequal access to mental health services, inadequate treatment, and lower quality of care for individuals with depression.

Personal Stories of Stigma

Personal stories provide powerful insights into the lived experiences of stigma and highlight the importance of addressing this issue. Here are a few narratives that shed light on the impact of stigma:

Elena's Experience: Battling Self-Stigma

Elena, a successful lawyer, struggled with depression for years before seeking help. She internalized the societal stigma, believing that admitting her struggles would be seen as a sign of weakness and incompetence.

"I felt like I had to keep up this façade of being strong and capable all the time," Elena recalls. "Admitting that I was struggling felt like admitting failure."

Elena's self-stigma prevented her from seeking help, and her depression worsened. It was not until a close friend encouraged her to see a therapist that she began to address her condition. Through therapy, Elena learned to challenge her self-stigma and recognize that seeking help was a sign of strength, not weakness.

"I realized that taking care of my mental health was just as important as taking care of my physical health," Elena says. "The support I received made a world of difference."

Jamie's Journey: Facing Workplace Discrimination

Jamie, a talented graphic designer, experienced severe depression following a personal loss. When Jamie confided in his manager about his struggles and requested some time off to seek treatment, he faced immediate discrimination.

"My manager told me that I needed to 'toughen up' and that taking time off would be seen as a lack of dedication," Jamie shares. "I felt completely unsupported and judged."

Feeling pressured to continue working despite his condition, Jamie's performance suffered, and he eventually left the job. His experience highlights the need for better workplace policies and greater understanding of mental health issues.

"No one should have to choose between their job and their mental health," Jamie asserts. "Workplaces need to be more supportive and accommodating."

Sophia's Story: Overcoming Public Stigma

Sophia, a university student, faced public stigma when she disclosed her depression to her classmates. Some peers responded with empathy, but others were dismissive or judgmental.

"People would say things like 'just snap out of it' or 'everyone feels sad sometimes,'" Sophia recalls. "It made me feel even more isolated and misunderstood."

Despite these challenges, Sophia found solace in a mental health support group on campus. Sharing her experiences with others who understood her struggles helped her feel less alone and empowered her to advocate for greater mental health awareness.

"Being part of the support group showed me that I'm not

alone," Sophia says. "It gave me the courage to speak out and challenge the stigma."

Advocating for Greater Understanding and Empathy

Addressing the stigma of depression requires collective effort and a multifaceted approach. Here are some strategies to promote greater understanding and empathy:

1. Education and Awareness

- **Public Campaigns**: National and community-level campaigns can raise awareness about depression and educate the public about its causes, symptoms, and treatments.
- **School Programs**: Incorporating mental health education into school curricula can help young people understand and address mental health issues from an early age.
- **Workplace Training**: Providing mental health training for employees and managers can create a more supportive work environment and reduce stigma.

2. Sharing Personal Stories

- **Lived Experiences**: Encouraging individuals to share their stories of depression can humanize the condition and challenge stereotypes.
- **Media Representation**: Promoting accurate and compassionate portrayals of mental health in the media can help shift public perception and reduce stigma.

3. Advocacy and Policy Change

- **Mental Health Legislation**: Advocating for policies that protect the rights of individuals with mental health conditions can reduce discrimination and improve access to care.
- **Workplace Policies**: Encouraging employers to adopt mental health-friendly policies, such as flexible work arrangements and mental health days, can create a more inclusive workplace.

4. Building Supportive Communities

- **Peer Support Groups**: Creating and promoting peer support groups can provide individuals with a safe space to share their experiences and receive support.
- **Community Programs**: Community-based programs that offer mental health resources and support can help reduce isolation and stigma.

5. Promoting Self-Compassion

- **Challenging Self-Stigma**: Helping individuals recognize and challenge their own self-stigmatizing beliefs can empower them to seek help and support.
- **Encouraging Self-Care**: Promoting self-care practices that prioritize mental health can help individuals manage their symptoms and improve their well-being.

Conclusion

The stigma associated with depression is a significant barrier to seeking help, receiving support, and achieving recovery. By addressing stigma through education, advocacy, and the sharing of personal stories, we can create a more understanding and empathetic society.

Breaking down the barriers of stigma requires collective action and a commitment to promoting mental health awareness and acceptance. By fostering a culture of empathy and support, we can ensure that individuals with depression feel valued, understood, and empowered to seek the help they need.

Together, we can challenge the misconceptions and discrimination surrounding depression and pave the way for a more compassionate and inclusive future. Through greater understanding and empathy, we can support the millions of individuals affected by depression and help them on their journey toward healing and recovery.

9

Hope and Healing

Depression can often feel like an unending darkness, where hope seems elusive and the future uncertain. However, countless stories of recovery and resilience demonstrate that healing is not only possible but attainable. This chapter offers hope through personal narratives of overcoming depression and highlights the potential for a brighter future beyond the struggle.

The Power of Hope

Hope is a vital component of recovery from depression. It provides the motivation to seek help, the strength to persevere through treatment, and the belief in a better tomorrow. Hope can be found in various forms: through the support of loved ones, the guidance of healthcare professionals, and the stories of others who have walked a similar path.

Personal Stories of Recovery

Emma's Story: Finding Light in the Darkness

Emma, a 35-year-old teacher, had been battling depression for most of her adult life. The overwhelming weight of her condition led her to isolate herself from friends and family. She felt trapped in a cycle of despair and hopelessness.

"My depression made me feel like I was drowning, and no one could see it," Emma recalls. "I didn't believe things could ever get better."

A turning point came when Emma's sister, Sarah, reached out with unwavering support and encouraged her to seek professional help. Emma began seeing a therapist who specialized in cognitive-behavioural therapy (CBT).

"Therapy helped me recognize and challenge the negative thought patterns that were fuelling my depression," Emma explains. "It wasn't an overnight change, but slowly, I started to see a glimmer of hope."

Emma's therapist also suggested joining a support group for individuals with depression. Through this group, Emma connected with others who understood her struggles and shared their own journeys toward healing.

"Hearing others' stories of recovery gave me hope," Emma says. "It made me realize that I wasn't alone, and that recovery was possible."

With the combination of therapy, support from her sister, and the encouragement of her support group, Emma gradually began to reclaim her life. She started to engage in activities she once enjoyed, reconnected with friends, and found new ways to cope with stress.

"I still have difficult days, but now I know that I can get through them," Emma reflects. "Hope has been my guiding light, and it has made all the difference."

Liam's Journey: Embracing Resilience

Liam, a 28-year-old musician, experienced a severe depressive episode following the loss of his mother. The grief and sadness overwhelmed him, and he struggled to find a way forward.

"I felt like I was stuck in a dark tunnel with no way out," Liam recalls. "I couldn't see a future without the pain."

Encouraged by a close friend, Liam sought help from a psychiatrist who diagnosed him with major depressive disorder. The psychiatrist prescribed medication to help manage his symptoms and recommended therapy to address his grief and depression.

"Starting medication was a difficult decision, but it was a crucial step in my recovery," Liam explains. "It helped stabilize my mood and gave me the clarity to work through my emotions in therapy."

Liam's therapist introduced him to mindfulness practices and encouraged him to express his feelings through music. Writing and performing songs became a therapeutic outlet for Liam, allowing him to process his grief and find solace in his passion.

"Music became my refuge," Liam says. "It allowed me to channel my pain into something meaningful and helped me heal."

Liam also found strength in connecting with others who had experienced similar losses. He joined a grief support group where he could share his story and listen to others, finding comfort in their shared experiences.

"Sharing my story and hearing others' journeys of resilience inspired me," Liam reflects. "It showed me that healing is possible, even after profound loss."

Over time, Liam's depression began to lift. He continued to work on his mental health through therapy, mindfulness, and music. With the support of his friend, therapist, and support group, Liam found hope and resilience.

"Recovery is a journey, not a destination," Liam says. "I've learned to embrace the ups and downs and find strength in my resilience."

Sophia's Transformation: From Struggle to Strength

Sophia, a 42-year-old entrepreneur, faced a series of personal and professional setbacks that led to a severe depressive episode. She felt overwhelmed by feelings of failure and worthlessness.

"Everything I had worked for seemed to be falling apart," Sophia recalls. "I didn't see a way out of the darkness."

Sophia's turning point came when a former colleague reached out and shared her own story of overcoming depression. Inspired by her colleague's resilience, Sophia decided to seek help.

"I realized that if she could find a way out, maybe I could too," Sophia explains. "It gave me the push I needed to seek professional help."

Sophia began seeing a therapist who used a combination of cognitive-behavioural therapy (CBT) and acceptance and commitment therapy (ACT). Through therapy, Sophia learned to challenge her negative beliefs and develop healthier coping strategies.

"My therapist helped me understand that my worth wasn't defined by my successes or failures," Sophia says. "It was a transformative realization."

Sophia also made significant lifestyle changes, incorporating regular exercise, a balanced diet, and mindfulness practices into her daily routine. These changes had a profound impact on her mental health.

"Taking care of my body and mind became a priority," Sophia reflects. "It helped me build a foundation for my recovery."

With the support of her therapist, former colleague, and new lifestyle habits, Sophia's depression began to lift. She regained her confidence and found new meaning in her life and work.

"Hope came from knowing that I had the strength to overcome my struggles," Sophia says. "It gave me the courage to keep moving forward."

The Potential for a Brighter Future

The stories of Emma, Liam, and Sophia demonstrate that recovery from depression is possible. Each person's journey is unique, but the common thread is the presence of hope, support, and resilience. These narratives offer a glimpse into the potential for a brighter future beyond depression.

Building a Foundation for Recovery

Several key elements can help build a foundation for recovery and a brighter future:

1. **Seeking Help**: Professional support, whether through therapy, medication, or both, is essential for managing depression and fostering recovery.
2. **Support Systems**: The encouragement and understanding of friends, family, and support groups can provide vital emotional and practical support.
3. **Self-Care**: Prioritizing self-care through healthy lifestyle choices, mindfulness practices, and activities that bring joy can enhance well-being and resilience.

4. **Hope and Positivity**: Cultivating hope and maintaining a positive outlook, even during challenging times, can provide the motivation to continue the journey toward recovery.

5. **Resilience and Adaptability**: Developing resilience and the ability to adapt to life's challenges can empower individuals to navigate setbacks and continue moving forward.

Looking Ahead

While the journey to recovery from depression can be long and challenging, it is important to remember that there is always hope. With the right support, treatment, and self-care, individuals can overcome depression and build a brighter future.

As society becomes more aware and understanding of mental health, the stigma associated with depression will continue to diminish. This cultural shift will create an environment where individuals feel empowered to seek help and share their stories, fostering a sense of community and support.

Conclusion

Hope and healing are not just distant dreams; they are attainable realities for those struggling with depression. Through the power of hope, the support of loved ones, and the resilience of the human spirit, recovery is possible.

The personal stories shared in this chapter highlight the strength and courage of individuals who have faced depression and emerged stronger. Their journeys offer inspiration and a reminder that, no matter how dark the path may seem, there is always a way forward.

By embracing hope, seeking help, and building a foundation for recovery, individuals with depression can look forward to a brighter future filled with possibility and potential. Together, we can create a world where hope and healing are within reach for everyone, and where the journey beyond depression leads to a life of fulfilment and joy.

10

Continuous Journey: Embracing Self-Care and Self-Discovery

Overcoming depression is not a one-time achievement or a destination; it is a continuous journey that requires ongoing effort, self-care, and self-discovery. Understanding this journey as a dynamic and evolving process helps individuals manage their mental health and build resilience for the future. This chapter explores the continuous nature of overcoming depression and emphasizes the importance of self-care and self-discovery in sustaining recovery.

The Nature of a Continuous Journey

Recovery from depression involves a series of steps, setbacks, and progressions. It is not a linear path, but a winding journey filled with challenges and triumphs. Acknowledging this can help individuals develop a realistic and compassionate approach to their mental health.

Recognizing Progress and Setbacks

Progress in overcoming depression can sometimes feel slow or imperceptible. It's important to celebrate small victories and recognize signs of improvement, such as:

- **Enhanced Mood Stability**: Experiencing more good days than bad ones.
- **Improved Relationships**: Reconnecting with friends and family.
- **Increased Engagement**: Participating in activities and hobbies that bring joy.
- **Greater Self-Awareness**: Developing insights into personal triggers and coping mechanisms.

Setbacks, such as a return of depressive symptoms or a difficult life event, are natural parts of the journey. Instead of viewing setbacks as failures, they can be seen as opportunities for growth and learning. Developing a resilient mindset helps in navigating these periods with greater ease.

Building Resilience

Resilience is the ability to adapt and bounce back from adversity. It is a crucial component of the continuous journey of overcoming depression. Building resilience involves:

- **Developing Coping Strategies**: Identifying and practicing effective ways to manage stress and emotional pain.
- **Strengthening Support Networks**: Cultivating relationships with people who provide emotional and practical

support.
- **Embracing Flexibility**: Being open to change and adaptable in the face of new challenges.
- **Fostering Optimism**: Maintaining a hopeful outlook and focusing on positive outcomes.

The Role of Self-Care in Sustaining Recovery

Self-care is essential in maintaining mental health and well-being. It involves intentional actions taken to nurture the mind, body, and spirit. Integrating self-care practices into daily life can help sustain recovery and prevent relapse.

Physical Self-Care

- **Exercise**: Regular physical activity has been shown to improve mood and reduce symptoms of depression. Finding enjoyable forms of exercise, such as walking, yoga, or dancing, can make it easier to incorporate into daily routines.
- **Nutrition**: A balanced diet that includes a variety of nutrients supports overall health and mental well-being. Staying hydrated and limiting the intake of processed foods and sugars can also positively impact mood.
- **Sleep**: Prioritizing good sleep hygiene is crucial for mental health. Establishing a regular sleep schedule, creating a restful environment, and practicing relaxation techniques before bed can improve sleep quality.

Emotional Self-Care

- **Therapy and Counselling**: Regular sessions with a therapist or counsellor provide ongoing support and a safe space to explore emotions and challenges.
- **Mindfulness and Meditation**: Practicing mindfulness and meditation can help reduce stress and increase emotional regulation. Techniques such as deep breathing, body scans, and guided imagery can be beneficial.
- **Journaling**: Writing about thoughts and feelings can offer clarity and insight. It can also serve as a therapeutic outlet for processing emotions.

Social Self-Care

- **Maintaining Connections**: Staying connected with supportive friends and family members is vital. Regular social interactions can provide emotional support and reduce feelings of isolation.
- **Setting Boundaries**: Learning to say no and setting healthy boundaries protect mental health and prevent burnout. It's important to prioritize personal needs and well-being.
- **Participating in Community**: Engaging in community activities, volunteer work, or support groups can foster a sense of belonging and purpose.

The Importance of Self-Discovery

Self-discovery is the process of gaining a deeper understanding of oneself. It involves exploring personal values, beliefs, passions, and goals. This journey of self-awareness and self-acceptance is integral to sustained recovery from depression.

Exploring Personal Values and Beliefs

Understanding and aligning with core values can provide direction and meaning in life. Reflecting on questions such as "What is truly important to me?" and "What do I want my life to stand for?" can guide decision-making and actions.

Identifying Passions and Interests

Engaging in activities that bring joy and fulfilment is essential for mental well-being. Exploring new hobbies, pursuing creative outlets, and participating in interests that spark passion can enhance life satisfaction.

Setting Goals and Aspirations

Setting realistic and meaningful goals provides motivation and a sense of purpose. Breaking down larger goals into smaller, manageable steps makes them more attainable and helps build confidence and momentum.

Practicing Self-Compassion

Self-discovery involves treating oneself with kindness and understanding. Practicing self-compassion means acknowledging imperfections and mistakes without judgment and recognizing the shared human experience of struggle and growth.

Embracing the Continuous Journey

The journey of overcoming depression is ongoing and requires continuous effort and adaptation. Embracing this journey involves:

- **Acceptance**: Accepting that mental health is a lifelong process and that difficulties are natural parts of the journey.
- **Commitment**: Committing to ongoing self-care practices and being proactive about seeking help when needed.
- **Growth Mindset**: Viewing challenges as opportunities for learning and personal growth.
- **Celebration**: Celebrating progress, no matter how small, and acknowledging the strength and resilience it takes to keep moving forward.

Conclusion

Overcoming depression is not a destination but a continuous journey of self-care and self-discovery. By recognizing the dynamic nature of this journey, individuals can approach their mental health with greater compassion and resilience.

Integrating self-care practices into daily life and engaging in the process of self-discovery are essential for sustaining recovery and building a fulfilling life. The stories of those who have navigated this journey remind us that, while the path may be challenging, it is also filled with opportunities for growth, joy, and hope.

Embracing the continuous journey means understanding that healing is an ongoing process that requires dedication and support. With the right tools, mindset, and community, individuals can navigate the difficulties of life with greater strength and find a brighter, more hopeful future beyond depression.

11

Encouragement for Others: Starting Your Journey to Overcome Depression

Starting the journey to overcome depression can be daunting and overwhelming, but it is also a courageous and transformative decision. This chapter offers encouragement, practical advice, and insights to support those who are beginning their journey toward healing and recovery.

Acknowledging Your Strength

Embarking on the journey to overcome depression requires immense strength and courage. It's important to recognize and acknowledge the bravery it takes to seek help and take steps towards better mental health. You are not alone in this journey, and there are resources and support systems available to assist you every step of the way.

Seeking Professional Help

One of the most important steps you can take is to seek professional help. A mental health professional, such as a therapist, counsellor, or psychiatrist, can provide you with the guidance, support, and tools necessary to manage your depression effectively. Here are some tips for finding the right professional:

- **Research and Referrals**: Ask for recommendations from friends, family, or your primary care physician. Research potential therapists or counsellors online and read reviews to find someone who specializes in treating depression.

- **Initial Consultation**: Schedule an initial consultation with a few therapists to see who you feel most comfortable with. It's important to find someone you trust and can openly communicate with.

- **Therapeutic Approach**: Different therapists may use different therapeutic approaches, such as cognitive-behavioural therapy (CBT), dialectical behaviour therapy (DBT), or psychodynamic therapy. Find out which approach resonates with you and aligns with your treatment goals.

Building a Support Network

Surround yourself with a supportive network of friends, family members, and peers who can provide emotional encouragement and practical assistance. Here's how you can cultivate a supportive environment:

- **Open Communication**: Share your thoughts and feelings with trusted individuals who can offer empathy and understanding. Expressing your emotions can help alleviate feelings of isolation and loneliness.

- **Join Support Groups**: Consider joining a support group for individuals with depression. Connecting with others who are going through similar experiences can provide validation, encouragement, and valuable insights.

- **Educate Your Support System**: Help your friends and family members understand depression by sharing resources and information. Encourage open dialogue about mental health to reduce stigma and foster a supportive environment.

Developing Self-Care Practices

Self-care is essential for maintaining mental well-being and supporting recovery from depression. Incorporate self-care practices into your daily routine to nurture your mind, body, and spirit:

- **Physical Activity**: Engage in regular exercise, such as walking, jogging, yoga, or dancing. Physical activity releases endorphins and improves mood.

- **Healthy Eating**: Eat a balanced diet rich in fruits, vegetables, whole grains, and lean proteins. Avoid excessive consumption of processed foods, sugars, and caffeine, which can negatively impact mood.

- **Quality Sleep**: Prioritize good sleep hygiene by establishing a consistent sleep schedule and creating a relaxing bedtime routine. Aim for seven to nine hours of sleep per night to support mental and emotional well-being.

- **Mindfulness and Relaxation**: Practice mindfulness meditation, deep breathing exercises, or progressive muscle relaxation to reduce stress and promote relaxation.

Setting Realistic Goals

Setting and achieving realistic goals can provide a sense of accomplishment and motivation on your journey to overcome depression. Start small and gradually work your way up to larger goals. Here's how to set achievable goals:

- **SMART Goals**: Use the SMART criteria (Specific, Measurable, Achievable, Relevant, Time-bound) to outline your goals. Break them down into smaller, manageable steps to track your progress.

- **Celebrate Progress**: Celebrate each milestone and accomplishment, no matter how small. Recognize your efforts and resilience in working towards your goals.

Coping with Setbacks

Recovery from depression is not a linear process, and setbacks may occur along the way. It's important to approach setbacks with compassion and resilience. Here are strategies for coping with setbacks:

- **Self-Compassion**: Practice self-compassion by being kind and understanding towards yourself during challenging times. Treat setbacks as opportunities for growth and learning.

- **Reach Out for Support**: Lean on your support network and mental health professionals for guidance and encouragement. Don't hesitate to seek help when you need it.

- **Review Your Coping Strategies**: Reflect on what coping strategies have been effective for you in the past and consider adjusting or trying new techniques.

Maintaining Hope and Persistence

Lastly, remember that healing from depression is a journey that requires patience, persistence, and perseverance. Maintain hope and trust in your ability to overcome challenges and build a fulfilling life. You can create positive change and finding joy and meaning in your life.

Conclusion

Starting your journey to overcome depression is a courageous and empowering decision. By seeking professional help, building a support network, practicing self-care, setting realistic goals, and cultivating resilience, you can take positive steps towards healing and recovery. Remember, you are not alone on this journey, and there are resources and communities ready to support you. Embrace the process, celebrate your progress, and continue moving forward with hope and determination, and together we will Guide the Black Dog Home.